ALL ABOUT AMA

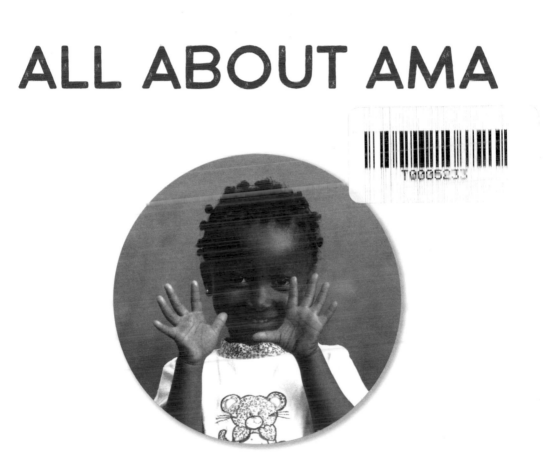

Kathy Knowles

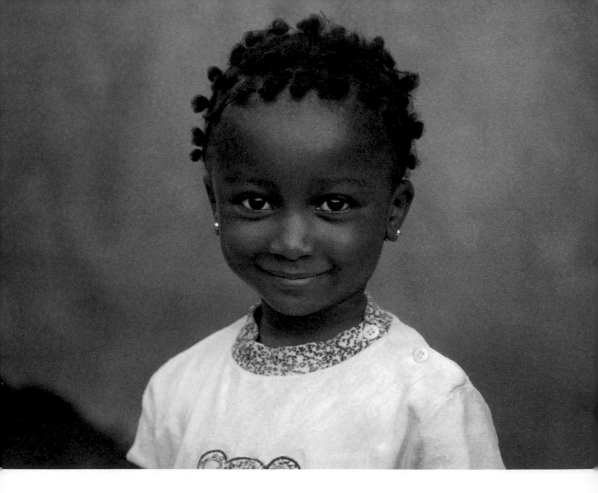

My name is Ama.

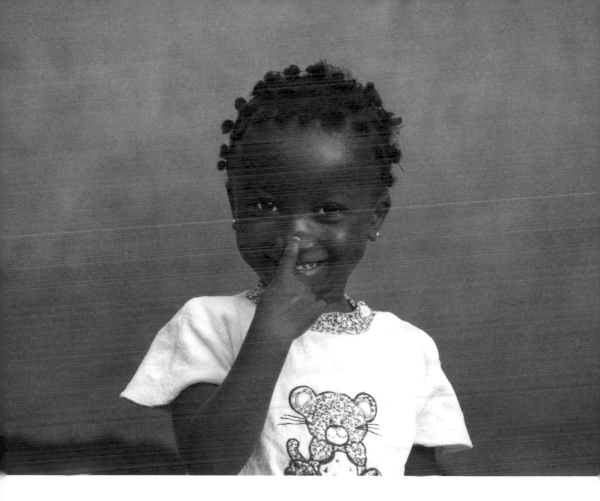

I have one nose.

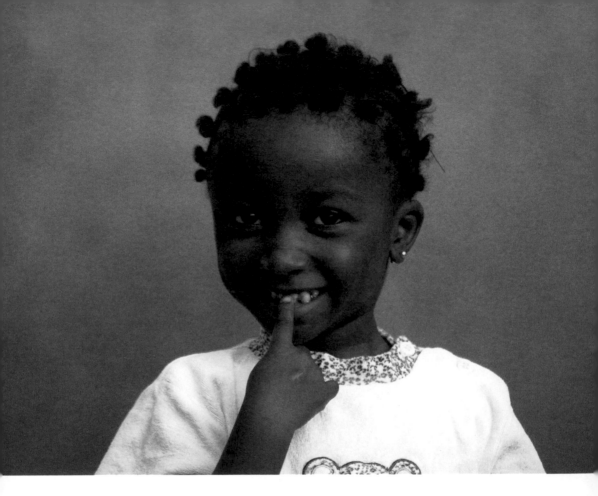

I have one mouth.

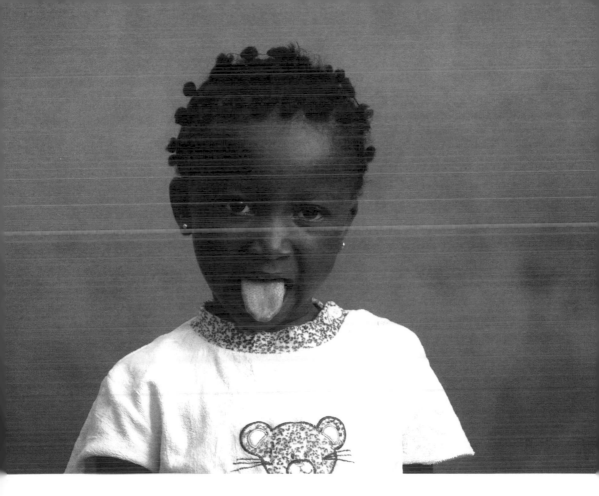

I have one tongue.

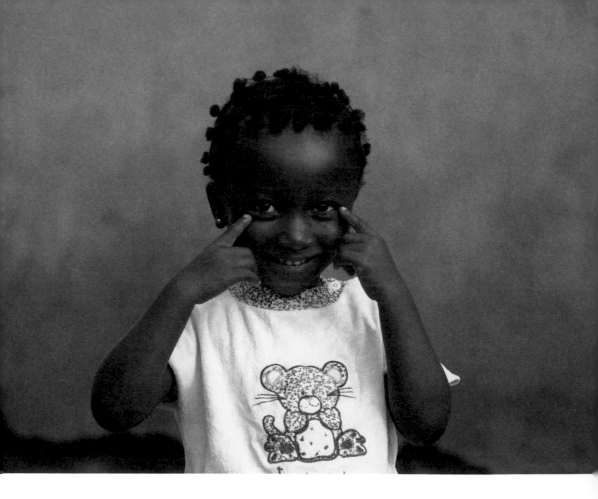

I have two eyes.

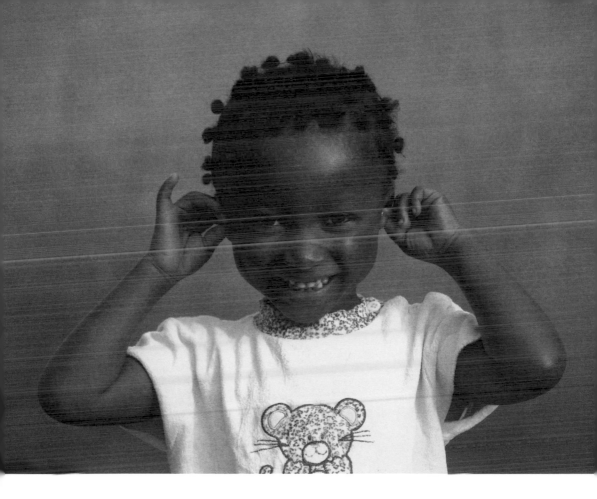

I have two ears.

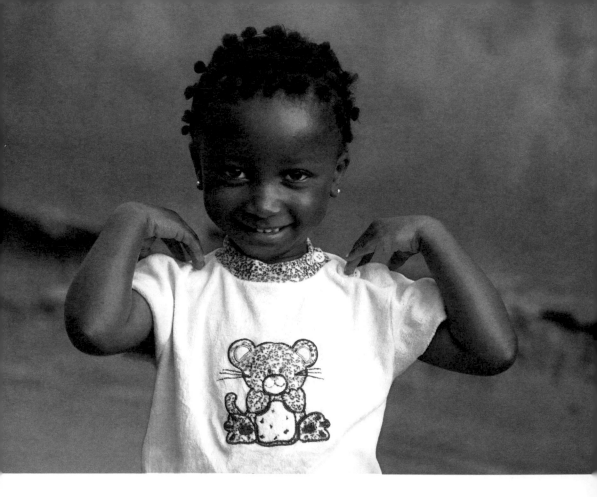

I have two shoulders.

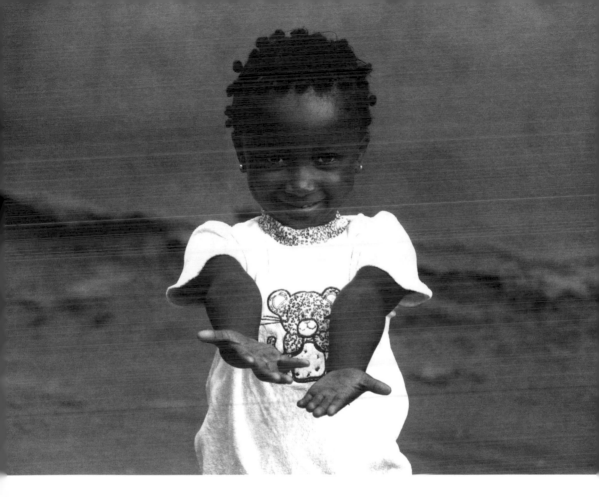

I have two arms.

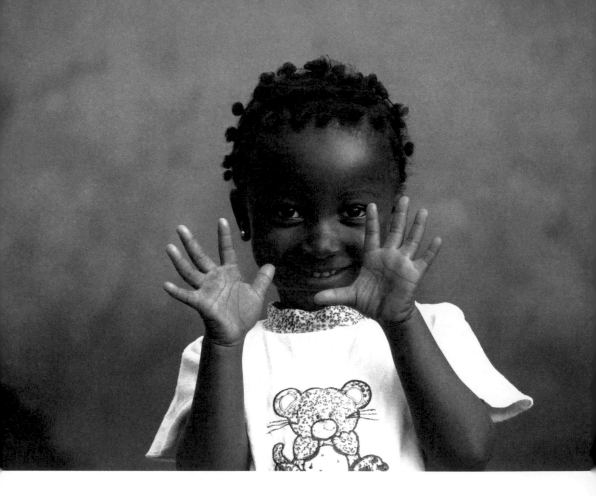

I have two hands.

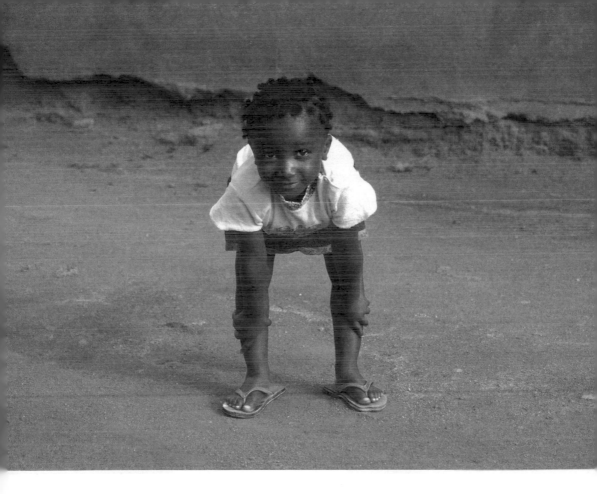

I have two legs.

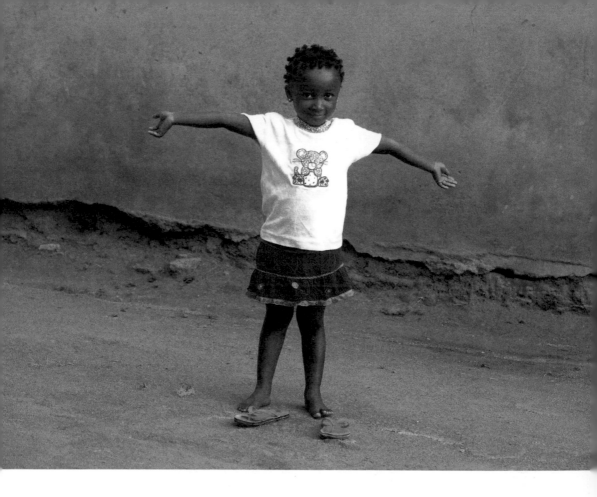

That is all of me!